THE
MAGICAL WORLD
OF HORSES

ADULT COLORING BOOK

CINDY ELSHAROUNI
TAMER ELSHAROUNI
VOLUME 2

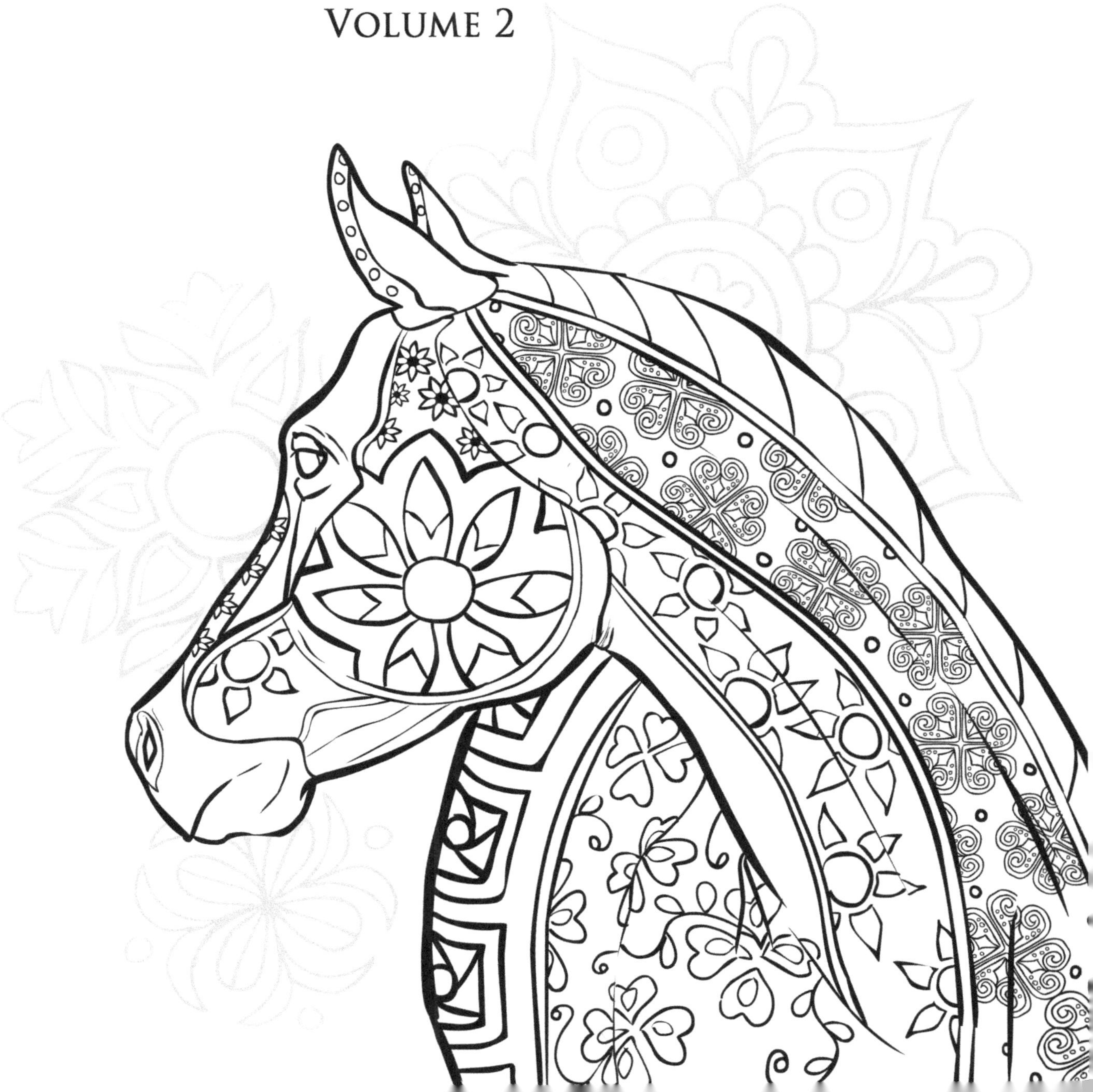

Published in 2016 by
Createspace
Email:tamercindy@selahworks.com
Website: www.selahworks.com
All rights reserved. No part of this book may be
reproduced in any form without written permission
of the copyright owners. If you would like to see more
images and stay updated on new coloring books,
visit our web page at www.selahworks.com or
facebook page https://www.facebook.com/AdultColoringBooksSelahWorks/

Cover Design by Cindy Elsharouni
Book Design Tamer Elsharouni

Printed in the U.S.A.

The Magical World Of Horses

This book combines two worlds into one. The magical world
of freedom, joy, love ,celebration and exhilaration
of the equine world comes together with the beautiful relaxing
process of creativity and individual expression. This is the
second volume of Cindy Elsharouni and
Tamer Elsharouni's equine adult coloring book.

This book contains 40 realistic equine related pages to color.
These pages will open a world of creative possibilities
and hours of enjoyment. Every image is a reflection of a
beautiful characteristic of the horse. The designs
and patterns are intricately added in an artistic manner
to only add to the beauty the horse already possesses.
Relax, enjoy and create some beauties.

FREE PDF PAGES FOR YOU!

_____

Go To This Link To Get Your Free Bonus PDF Pages

https://selahworks.thrivecart.com/magical-world-of-horses-bonus

I will be adding more pages over time to this link just for you,
so stay updated through my facebook page
www.facebook.com/AdultColoringBooksSelahWorks

The full PDF of this book is sold seperately.

  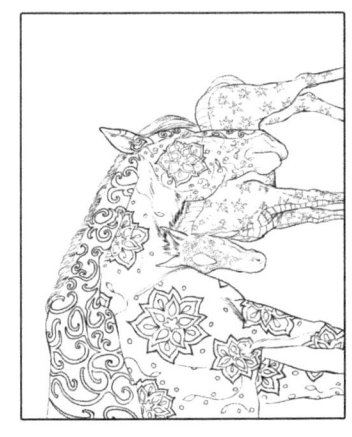 

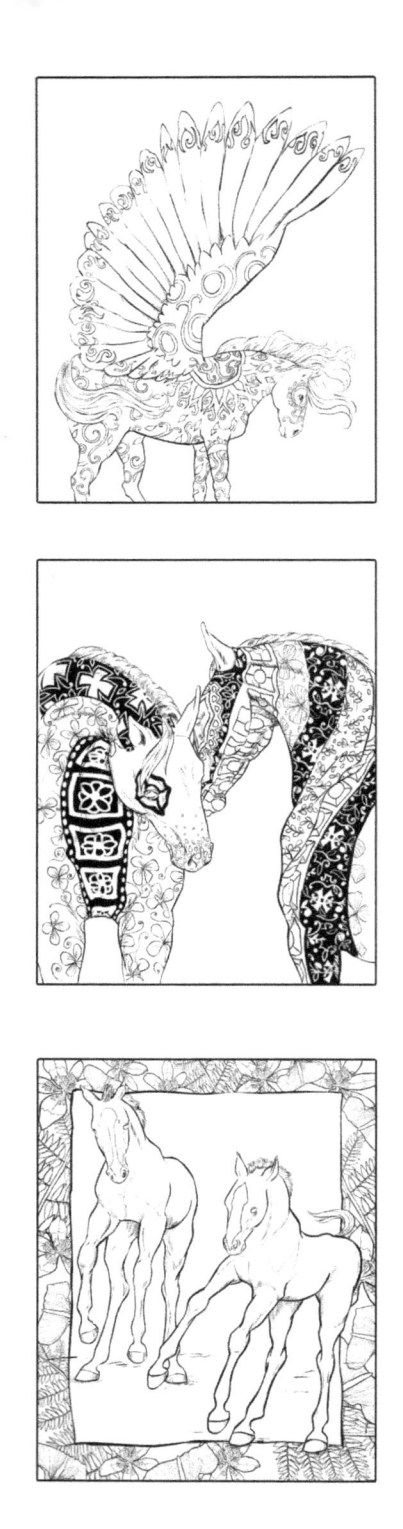

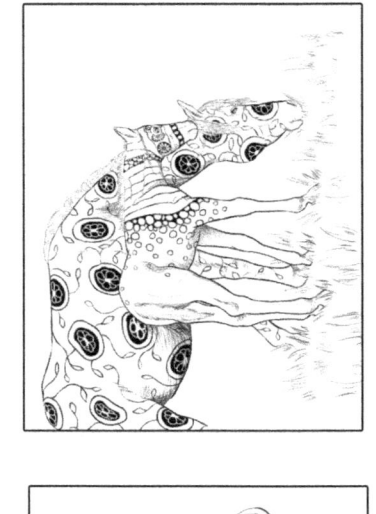

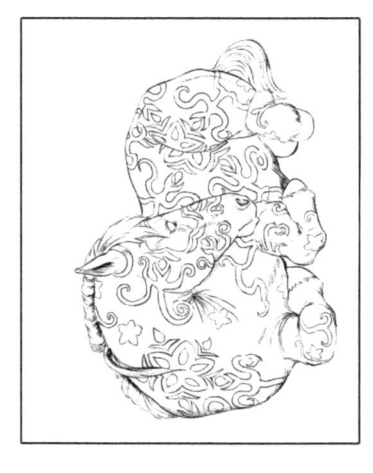

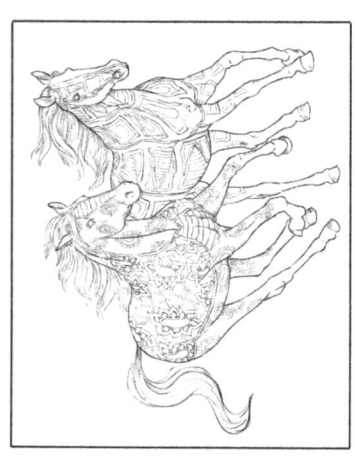

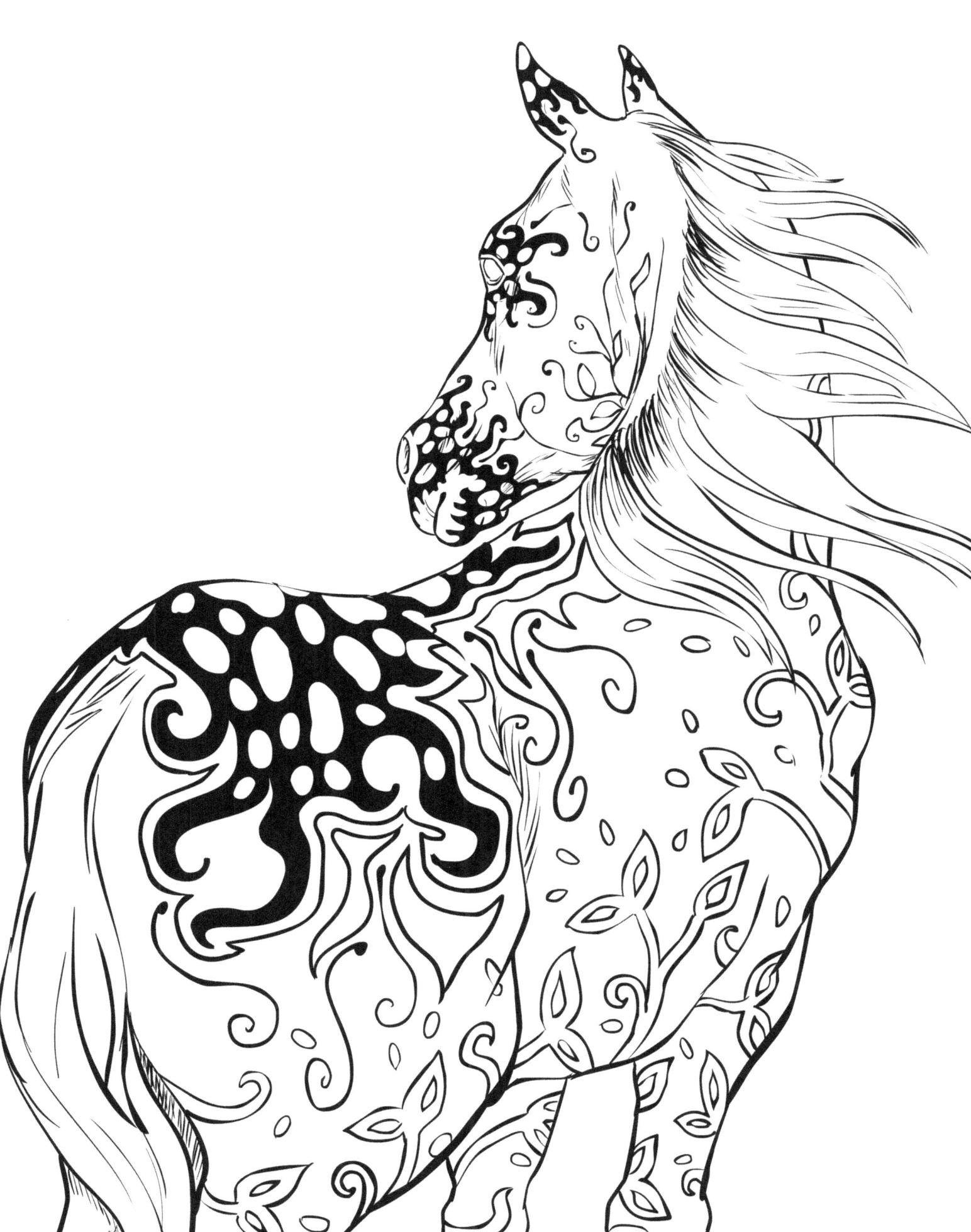

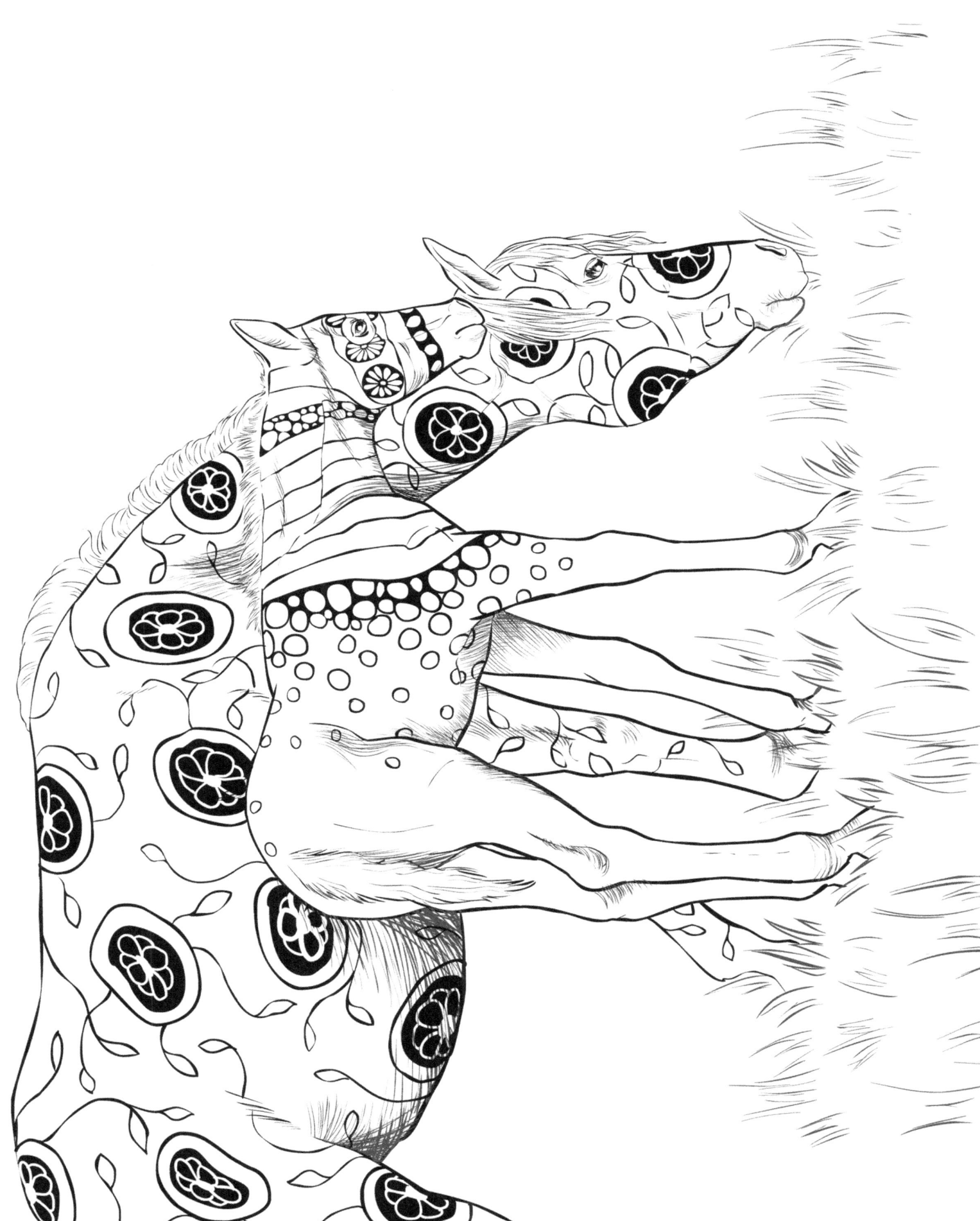

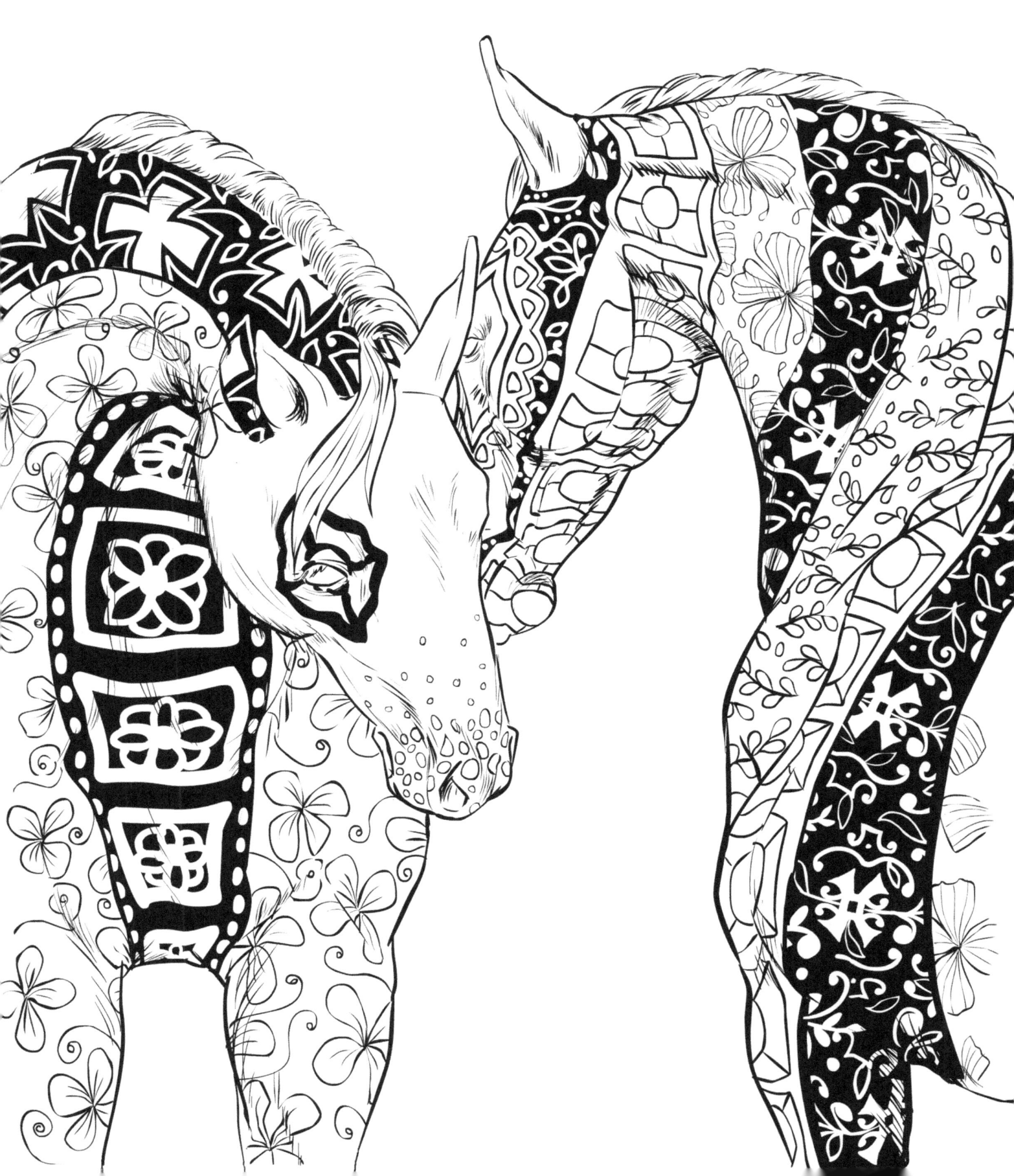

MORE BOOKS BY CINDY ELSHAROUNI!
IF YOU LOVE HORSES, DOGS OR JUST WANT
A COLLECTION OF ANIMALS,
DON'T MISS OUT ON THESE BOOKS.

AVAILABLE ON AMAZON.COM OR WWW.SELAHWORKS.COM

About the Artists

Cindy Elsharouni has been drawing since the age of three. She has developed into a professional fine artist and has held multiple exhibitions internationally. Her main subject matter almost always incorporates animals or humans, particularly faces of people of different backgrounds and walks of life different from her own. She loves to create artwork that has significant meaning and that speaks a message to the viewer.

Tamer Elsharouni is also an achieved professional artist, graduated from the faculty of Fine Arts in Cairo, who has art obtained by collectors worldwide and has his artwork displayed internationally. He has held innumerable private exhibitions and international art awards. He also has a passion to create artwork that impacts people and society as a whole. He speaks at conferences and seminars internationally equipping other artists.

Tamer and Cindy now work on projects together. They have put together this book as an endeavor to allow others who don't like to label themselves as artists, to take part in an artistic process. They believe everyone has the potential to be an artist. Anyone can create in a form of expression.

Together, when possible, they finish off each other's work and also enjoy critiquing each other's work. They hope you enjoy the images in this book but even more so the process.